A little

ESSEX

Personal memories inspired by The Francis Frith Collection®

THE FRANCIS FRITH COLLECTION

www.francisfrith.com

Based on a book first published in the United Kingdom in 2013 by The Francis Frith Collection®

This edition published exclusively for Bradwell Books in 2013
For trade enquiries see: www.bradwellbooks.com or tel: 0800 834 920
ISBN 978-1-84589-725-3

British Library Cataloguing in Publication Data

A Little Book of Essex Memories
Personal Memories inspired by the Francis Frith Collection

The Francis Frith Collection
6 Oakley Business Park,
Wylye Road, Dinton,
Wiltshire SP3 5EU
Tel: +44 (0) 1722 716 376
Email: info@francisfrith.co.uk
www.francisfrith.com

Printed and bound in Malaysia
Contains material sourced from responsibly managed forests

Front Cover: Brentwood, Warley Road 1906 53503p
Frontispiece: Rochford, Stanbridge Mill c1955 R226011

The colour-tinting is for illustrative purposes only, and is not intended to be historically accurate

AS WITH ANY HISTORICAL DATABASE, THE FRANCIS FRITH ARCHIVE IS CONSTANTLY BEING
CORRECTED AND IMPROVED, AND THE PUBLISHERS WOULD WELCOME INFORMATION ON
OMISSIONS OR INACCURACIES

A little book of Memories – A Dedication

This book has been compiled from a selection of the thousands of personal memories added by visitors to the Frith website and could not have happened without these contributions. We are very grateful to everyone who has taken the time to share their memories in this way. This book is dedicated to everyone who has taken the time to participate in the Frith Memories project.

It is comforting to find so many stories full of human warmth which bring back happy memories of "the good old days". We hope that everyone reading this book will find stories that amuse and fascinate whilst at the same time be reminded of why we feel affection for Britain and what makes us all British.

Francis Frith always expressed the wish that his photographs be made available to as wide an audience as possible and so it is particularly pleasing to me that by creating the Frith web site we have been able to make this nationally important photographic record of Britain available to a worldwide audience. Now, by providing the Share Your Memories feature on the website we are delighted to provide an opportunity for members of the public to record their own stories and to see them published (both on the website and in this book), ensuring that they are shared and not lost or forgotten.

We hope that you too will be motivated to visit our website and add your own memories to this growing treasure trove – helping us to make it an even more comprehensive record of the changes that have taken place in Britain in the last 100 years and a resource that will be valued by generations to come.

John M Buck
Managing Director
www.francisfrith.com

The Witchfinder General's reign of terror

Essex has the unhappy distinction of having executed more witches than any other county in England's history, and the first major trial for witchcraft itself, as the main indictment, took place in Chelmsford in 1566 when 63-year-old Agnes Waterhouse of Hatfield Peverell was found guilty and hanged. One of the most unpleasant characters in the county's story was Matthew Hopkins, who lived at Manningtree in north-east Essex in the mid 17th century. After denouncing his crippled neighbour as a witch, Hopkins realised he had a particular talent for terrorising old women that could make him powerful and wealthy. He claimed to hold the 'Devil's own list of all the witches in England', and as the hysteria of witch-fever gripped East Anglia in 1645-46, many towns paid him to come and search for 'witches'. He assumed the title of 'Witchfinder General', made his headquarters in Colchester, and is believed to have been responsible for the deaths of up to 400 people throughout East Anglia; people were either denounced by neighbours (who were rewarded for the information) or tortured until they confessed, and were put to death for witchcraft on the most flimsy evidence. His reign of terror at last came to an end when John Gaule, a Huntingdonshire parson, decided that enough was enough and it was time Hopkins received his come-uppance. He preached a number of scathing sermons denouncing Hopkins and published his sermons in a pamphlet in which he attacked Hopkins and his accomplices, particularly denouncing his methods of obtaining 'confessions' by means of torture which, as he pointed out, was actually illegal in England at that time. His complaints helped lead to Hopkins being formally questioned about his methods, after which he retired from witch hunting and went home to Manningtree, where he died soon after, probably in 1647. He was buried at Mistley Heath, but that isn't the last of the story – his ghost is said to haunt the area around Mistley pond, particularly at the time of the full moon…

Julia Skinner

My ancestress was one of the Witches of Manningtree

I have visited Manningtree only once, but I have an interest in the area as my father (Donald Turner) is tracing our family tree and he has discovered that one of our ancestors – Elizabeth Goodwin – was tried and hanged as one of the witches of Manningtree that were 'discovered' by Matthew Hopkins! She was accused of casting a spell on a grocer's horse, and making it die, after he refused to give her credit to buy cheese.

Ann Martin

Manningtree, South Street c1955 M127021

Memories of Hythe Quay

In the late 1950s I spent much time at Hythe Quay at Colchester watching the shipping. First I would go to the library in Culver Street to look at the Lloyds news sheet to see which boats were arriving or leaving. I would also look up the details of the ships in the Lloyds Register. I remember the smell of petrol being unloaded and the slightly obnoxious smell from the works on the quayside that made firebricks. Ellis & Everard coasters were many of the ships that used the quay, the names of all their ships ended in '-ity' except their sailing barge the 'Will Everard'. The ships bringing the clay to the firebrick works were all Dutch.

David Adams

Colchester, Hythe Quay c1955 C136309

Happy Summer Days at the Pool

When I saw this photograph on the Frith website it reminded me of those carefree summer days in my childhood when we would cycle from Myland to the pool, leave our bikes unlocked in a heap outside, pay our 6d and go to the dank, cold, changing room under the bridge. We then spent many hours sunbathing and swimming, later to retrieve our bikes, intact, from beneath the pile.

The girls had to cross the end of the pool by a boardwalk to their changing room on the other side. There were high diving boards so the pool was about ten feet deep at the deep end. We discovered that there was a hole in the underwater wire netting beneath the boardwalk where we could dive down to come up under the boardwalk and bang on the boards as the girls walked over.

Sadly, the pool is now closed. I'm sure the modern pools nowadays are nowhere near as much fun as that outdoor pool at Colnebank.

Peter Gant

Colchester, The Swimming Pool c1960 C136042

The Ghostly Roman Soldier at Colchester

My Nanna who lived in Butt Road at Colchester had a few scary stories up her sleeve to thrill us with when I was a child, and one of them was about this old bit of wall, I don't remember it being fenced off when I was a girl. Anyway, she used to say that there was an old Roman soldier who used to walk the wall and appear at this gate, it still gives me a little shudder even today! My modern children are not at all interested in this little story, needless to say!

Wendy Nolan

Colchester, Old Roman Wall 1892   31530

My Grandfather Fred Scales

I was born in Brightlingsea and spent most of my childhood growing up there. My grandfather was Fred Scales, who ran the Boating Lake for a number of years and looked after the holiday chalets and caravans, he was also a coal merchant and lived in Colne Road. My grandfather is the man standing by the boats in this photograph!

Jennifer Dance

"My grandfather is the man standing by the boats in this photograph!"

Brightlingsea, The Boating Lake c1960 B209019

Memories of Point Clear Bay near St Osyth in the 1950s and 60s

My family and I used to spend our holidays at Point Clear almost every year during the late 1940s, 50s and 60s, and often met the same families each time we went down there. I remember one year in the mid 1950s when a neighbour's daughter and myself walked out to 'Anchor Island' (a sand island just offshore). It was a hot night so we decided to have a late night swim, but when we went to wade back, the tide had come in and had cut us off from the mainland. We made an attempt to reach higher ground, but the current swept us both along the island. Reaching the firm ground we became marooned; the incident finished up with the Clacton lifeboat putting out to sea to rescue us, it was very embarrassing!

Robert Munn

St Osyth, Point Clear Bay from the Martello Tower c1955 S38063

My year at Fingringhoe – 1944 to 1945

In 1944 my mother and I had just returned to England from South Africa, and we went to live in the Hall at Fingringhoe. My aunt was Nellie Combes who was the cook there and my mother was Doris Harrington who cleaned the rooms. Fingringhoe Hall was owned by Major Feaurneux and Mrs Feaurneux, who ran the farm. Mr Sturgeon was the man who looked after the cows and the large bull named 'Plonkey'. I helped find the chickens' eggs as the chickens were free range and laid most of their eggs in the local churchyard! My mother had fits when she saw me carrying two large baskets of eggs.

My first Christmas at the Hall was one I remember to this day. There was a large Christmas tree at the bottom of the staircase, with presents for the village children underneath. As I lived there I was allowed to choose two presents for myself. I had a game of draughts and a torch.

I went to the stone school at Fingringhoe next door to St Andrew's Church, where we were taught in one large room by a lady and some of the older pupils. I also remember going for haircuts during my time in the village. As there was no barber in Fingrinhoe, we had to walk a long way to get a ferry boat over to Wivenhoe – it was rowed with a pair of oars, there was no motor in those days. We used to have one bus a week into Colchester, returning in the afternoon. When the Second World War came to an end my father, who had been a POW in Germany, came and stayed at the Hall to build himself up before we left and returned to London to live.

Derek Harrington

Holidays at Jaywick Sands

I went to Jaywick for a holiday way back in 1958. I went with my Mum, Dad and two younger sisters. The holiday chalets where we stayed were built on stilts along roads all named after British car manufacturers that are now long gone, such as Humber, Triumph and Riley – our road was Riley Avenue. There was a very small games arcade, the Everly Brothers, Chuck Berry and Duane Eddy were on the juke box, and Mum and Dad went to the club house most evenings. On the last night of our holiday, Mum and Dad were in a pub called 'The Never Say Die' and us kids sat outside with a lemonade and packet of crisps. There was a spectacular electric storm out to sea, with sheet and forked lightening lighting up the sky, and we watched this fantastic sight in awe. In the morning we found that the newly-erected flood defence barriers had been breached and the whole place was flooded, under about 3 feet of water – now we knew why the chalets had been built on stilts! We made our way back to the train station and headed back to London. This all seems a lifetime ago now.

Frank Torpey

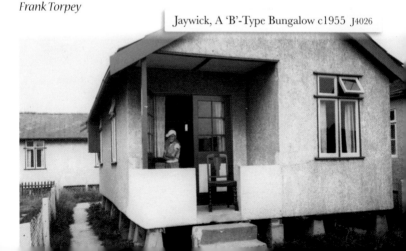

Jaywick, A 'B'-Type Bungalow c1955 J4026

I was the local equivalent of a Thomson's holiday guide

I absolutely loved the Jaywick of my childhood. The sun was always shining and our lives were so happy. I was perhaps luckier than most kids in the 1950s. My mum and dad owned several of the money-making properties in the area and I used to help them to make sure that the holidaymakers had a great time. I used to get up at 5 o'clock on a Saturday morning and go down to the coach station and wait for the arrivals from London. They always seemed to be on Suttons Coaches. I used to carry people's luggage for them and they gave me a few

> "Most of them used to say "What a dump" when they first arrived at Jaywick, but when I collected their luggage on their way home they could not praise up our little place enough."

bob for my services. There are people still out there who must remember me. I was called Snowy, I had blonde hair and was as brown as Nuggets Knocker, and was permanently in a bathing cossie and pushing my barrow. I was the local equivalent of a Thomson's holiday guide, and was only too pleased to tell the people the best places to go for a good laugh. Jaywick is still the same old place that we all loved, nothing much has changed.

Joe Fordham

Blissful days on the Amusements at Clacton!

This picture takes me back! It was around 1962 and I was 11 years old. We travelled down to Clacton from South Harrow on a Valiant Cronshaw coach, which we caught outside a pub in Northolt – The Plough, I think it was. We had a great journey to Clacton, and when we got there we stayed at 92 Rosemary Road.

Apart from a massive thunderstorm, the amusements and the beach were the main attractions and memories for me. On the way to the pier there were many arcades. I recall having to throw wooden balls up a 'bowling' alley with netting on each side. You were aiming for the middle hole, like a target, and if the ball went in there it was the highest score – registered by a black and white counter on top. If you got outer holes then you scored less points. The balls were noisily returned down a side chute. There were many other machines, such as the Ghost House where you put in a 1d and you saw spooky things happening in a glass case. My dad taught me the shooting targets game. You put in 6d and if you shot all 20 targets (quite difficult!), then you got your 6d back.

The pier had fast dodgems with no bumping allowed – the forerunner of go-carts. And there were the ordinary boring ones too that went slowly. The Steel Stella big dipper towered above on the pier but I wasn't brave enough to go on it. The noise of the chains and cars running down the tracks could be heard all over Clacton seafront. Happy days!

Paul Starck

Clacton-on-Sea, The Pier and the Steel Stella 1958 C107062

Such Great Holidays!

I remember as a child having great family holidays in the 1960s on the beaches at Holland-on-Sea. We hired a beach hut for 7/6 a week, near the deck chair and paddle float hire. We used to try and climb the concrete wall going back up to the road near the First Aid hut as a dare. Perhaps that's why it was put there! I remember the cafés on the beach, and who can forget the pretty girls who pushed the ice-cream trolleys up and down the prom calling out "Wall's Ices!". We stayed at Valley Farm where in the evenings we were entertained by Ronnie Mills and his band. The highlight of those evenings was doing the 'March of the Mods' on the dance floor and the talent competition. They were such great times.

Kevin Chapple

Holland-on-Sea, The Sands c1960 H177097

I was one of those pretty Walls ice-cream girls!

I saw Mr Chapple's memory about Holland-on-Sea (opposite) on the Frith website, where he mentioned the Walls ice-cream girls and how pretty they were – I was one of those girls, and I can't quite believe that someone has written about us! What fun we had. We all worked in the school holidays in the beach cafés, it was hard work sometimes but we had such good times. The beaches were packed and we sold lots of Walls ices! The concrete face on the cliffs down to the beach was the source of much competition as we all tried to climb it from the bottom to the top. It was more fun, however, in the winter when there was ice on it – we were so daring!   *Liz Croxon*

Childhood pranks at Holland-on-Sea in the 1940s

I am Duncan Burrett, a twin whose brother was Paul, and we had a little sister Barbara. My dad bought the Naze Park Laundry at Holland-on-Sea when we were 4 years of age. I have many memories of the time we spent there but the one that particularly sticks in my mind is when my sister fell down a deep well in the garden – or should I say when she was pushed down it, probably by my brother because she wouldn't let him ride her bike. Dr Johnson was quick on the scene after my Uncle Andy rescued her from the bottom of the well, which was filthy and full of rubbish, bricks and glass. She was OK though. I also remember when Paul and I went to the local Regal Cinema and fell asleep. When we woke up the place was dark and locked up, as no one had seen us there when they locked the cinema for the night. My brother began to cry, so we went into the foyer and helped ourselves to some sweets to cheer us up. Eventually my Auntie Joan, who worked there in the ticket office, arrived with the police and let us out.   Duncan Burrett

Growing up in Finchingfield

My family, Ken and Joan Blake, owned the Church Hill Stores in Finchingfield (opposite the church) from 1945 to the early 1950s, then we lived in the village until 1957. I have many memories of my time in Finchingfield and many faces and events came flooding back when I saw the Finchingfield photos on the Frith website. This picture shows a row of cottages known to me as The Causeway where in my time there was an ice-cream shop. The lane opposite, called The Pikle (I'm not sure of the correct spelling), had high brick walls on both sides and as a child I used to stamp along there in my Wellington boots, making a lovely echoing plonk. I can still hear the sound.

Lesley Alexander

Finchingfield, Old Cottages c1960   F77027

Happy times in Thaxted

We came to live in Thaxted in about 1950, and though we lived in one of the Borough Cottages in Bolford Street, which then were in a bad state, for me, fresh out of an institution (I was only eight), it was the most wonderful place – and I still feel that way about it. I had my own bedroom, and though all it held was a brass-knobbed bedstead and a wash-bowl, it was MINE and I could see the beauty of the world from it. I remember Farmer Latham, and the windmill, which was in a less finished state than now, and the morris dancers, and seeing the wind ripple the grain in the fields, and the barn that got burned down, next to the pigsties. I used to play in the stream next to the barn, and on the old army lorry in the back garden, and the tractor quietly rusting in the front. Oh, and I loved to see the stars and hear the owls screeching at night. Without doubt my entire childhood started and stopped in that place – and I was so sad when we had to move away.   *Pat Weedon*

Thaxted, The Almshouses and the Windmill c1955   T28016

A patient's view of Saffron Walden General Hospital in 1953

When I was eight I was admitted to Saffron Walden General Hospital for surgery. My parents were told that I would be discharged home at the end of the week. I vividly remember the feeling of being suffocated when the pad of chloroform was put over my face to anaesthetise me. During the week a young girl was admitted to the ward with suspected Polio. She was put into a glass-encased cubicle and the next day she was transferred to the isolation hospital. It was decided that all the children in the ward should be put into quarantine for three weeks, so my week turned into four! Visiting hours were restricted to a short time in the afternoon on Tuesdays, Thursdays and at the weekends as it was considered unsettling for children to see their parents more frequently! The weeks seemed very long. However, it obviously didn't affect me too adversely as ten years later I trained to be a SRN (State Registered Nurse). In later years an extension was added to the hospital building and it is now the home of the local council offices.

Mrs H L Sharpe

Saffron Walden, The Hospital 1932 85119

Fun at the 'Paddler' in Saffron Walden in the 1960s

I have lived in Saffron Walden all my life of 50 years and have many great memories of the town. My greatest memories are of the time we had at the locally named 'Paddler'. The Paddler was at the top end of Rowntree Way. The area had a pumping station owned by the Water Board (which is still there today). There was a large paddling pool there and the area was a favourite place for families to go and have picnics and a swim on a hot summer Sunday. There were also two large grass play areas (which are no longer there due to houses being built on the site). In one corner of the biggest grass play area was a large tree, you had to climb part of that tree if you wanted to be in one of the children's gangs that existed then. All the lads would play football on the grassy areas, using coats and bags as goalposts. The teams were usually picked by which part of Rowntree Way you lived in, Upper or Lower. As the Paddler got more and more popular, with more families coming from other parts of town, more boys wanted to play football, so it was decided to form a league between ourselves. Then other teams were invited to join and we held tournaments every so often. When England won the World Cup in 1966 it was football every day for weeks, with everyone wanting to be the England team and their players. The Paddler was a great place for all the family.

Ian Lench

My friend Ginger...

We arrived in Wendens Ambo (two miles south-west of Saffron Walden) around 1953, and took up residence in a little cottage in the grounds of a big house. Opposite was a pond in which moorhens spent peaceful days. Next to the pond was a field – I think it is a play area and park now. One of my enduring memories is of a grey horse that grazed in that field. He and I had a wonderful relationship. I would lie on the ground and he would munch the grass peacefully nearby, and when I wandered off and saw some juicer spot he would come and graze there if I called him. I can even remember being underneath his giant belly, with no fear that he would tread on me. One day a man came to the fence and leaned on it, and when the horse saw this man, he suddenly charged off and started snorting and leaping near to the man. The man moved away and must have gone in to see my mother, for I was told that I must not go in the field again as the horse was 'dangerous'. The strangest thing is, I think that horse and I had actually met a year or two before, and in quite a different place, and had then struck up a very special relationship. Why do I think that? Well how many flea-bitten grey old milk horses do you see with a curly mustache whose name is 'Ginger'? My other memories of the village are of the church, and going to get a stone jar of something from the shop, but losing the money before I got there, and the stream, and lying in bed one evening and seeing this dark blob on the ceiling above me and wondering if it was a spider – and it was, and it fell and plopped onto my pillow. I have never moved as fast as then! Soon we were on the move again and the next place where I lived was ugly – but Wendens Ambo was beautiful.

Pat Weedon

A little book of memories

Living at the Mill in Felsted

My father bought the mill at Felsted in the 1960s and we moved
away in 1976 to South Africa. We all have plenty of memories of
the years we spent living there. The most memorable was the
first time we encountered the ghost of the mill. My mother
called my two brothers and sister and myself into the hallway
and demanded to know who had been playing the grand piano
in the main lounge. We were not allowed in there so she was not
impressed that we had broken the rules. We all looked at each
other in amazement. Suddenly we heard the piano music again.
Mother, armed with a brass poker stick in hand, went with all of us
into the main lounge. To our surprise no one was in there. It was a
bit creepy at first but after a while we all got used to hearing the
music. It was a woman who used to play on the grand piano, and it
was beautiful soothing music that came from the room.

Christina Bryan

Felsted, The Mill c1960 F76015

More ghosts at the Mill

I also lived in the mill at Felsted, from 1978 to 1982 with my parents, brother and sister. I was only five when I left but I have memories of seeing a lady and man both dressed in very old-fashioned clothes around the mill pond, and nobody ever saw them except me. I'm sure they were looking after me and making sure I didn't fall in the water.

It was a very creepy house and I remember our dog, Polly, would go mad in the hall at night. When we left the mill, my mum went back one day and saw some builders inside it, doing the house up. My mum asked to look around but they told her to hurry as they didn't ever stay there in the dark. My

> "They told her to hurry as they didn't ever stay there in the dark."

mum asked why not, and they said it was because they had heard children screaming and a huge bang as if someone had fallen down the stairs in the hall. They went outside, thinking some children might be in the drive, but there was nobody around. I'm thinking our dog knew something happened in the hall.

Victoria Brock

Memories of Braintree County High School in the 1940s

I attended Braintree County High School from 1944 to 1950. 'Nihil Nisi Optima' I recall was the school motto, and the school song started with the words 'With hearts close knit in comradeship …'. I remember some joker during Morning Assembly changing the words to the last two lines of the first verse to: 'And, welcome him with half a brick, Who talks of school and arithmetic.' Giggling during Assembly was highly frowned upon by the headmaster, Dr Cordingly. Thus, one morning after

> "Two friends of mine and I were summoned to receive 'six of the best'!"

dropping a water bomb during prayers from the balcony above the Assembly Hall in the main building, two friends of mine, Robin Addington and Gordon Smee, and I were summoned to receive 'six of the best'!

Roy Stone

Braintree, County High School 1907 57571

Great Waltham, Chelmsford Road c1965   G101005

I was the village policeman at Great Waltham

In the late 1950s I was the village policeman at Great Waltham. The police house was the last two-storied house at the Barrack Land end of Cherry Garden Road with my 'office' being in the kitchen and the table there was my desk. My duties in those days were not very onerous, consisting mainly of attending motor accidents, moving on camping Gypsies and paying occasional visits to the local pubs in Great and Little Waltham, Howe Street and Mashbury. My means of getting around was on a bicycle, although about once a month a police car from Chelmsford would come to Great Waltham and I would act as observer for a couple of hours. My immediate superior officer was Sergeant Leslie Pye from Broomfield who was always very keen for us village policemen (including the one at Ford End (Constable Tom Mitchell) and Great Leighs (Constable Les Smith) to catch the local poacher by the name of Moore, who styled himself 'The King of the Poachers'. The squire was J J Tufnell who lived in the big house on the Langley estate, and in the garage he had a well polished Rolls Royce.

John Butcher

Harlow

Harlow as we know it today was the first London-area 'New Town' to result from the Town and Country Planning Act of 1946, a long-term plan to build a number of new towns around London to ease the housing crisis after the Second World War, when thousands of London families had lost their homes. The small village that was there before the new town arrived is known as Old Harlow, just to the east of the modern town. The new town of Harlow was developed from 1949 onwards on the site of four sparsely-inhabited parishes, a little to the west of the 'old town' of Harlow. So many young families moved to Harlow New Town that in the 1960s it was given the nickname of 'Pram Town' because of the number or prams and pushchairs that could be seen there.

Julia Skinner

Old Harlow, Churchgate Street 1903 51086

No paths – a memory of the new town
of Harlow from 1958

I can remember moving into our house in Rivermill in
Harlow new town in 1958. The houses had only just been
built. There were no paths leading up to the houses or
pavements and roads. It was a wonderful feeling even for a
child of three to be walking into a freshly-built house that
no one else had lived in.

Janet James

Harlow, Broad Walk c1960 H22083

Harlow Market

I remember the café in the market square at Harlow in the 1960s, my mum used to work in the open top part in the summer and my brother and I would help her clear the tables when we were on school holidays. I remember the shops that ran around the top of the square, especially the barber's shop where my brother would have his hair cut, 'short back and sides and not too much off the top'. I also remember going to the market at Christmas time when my mum got her money from the Christmas club she belonged to, and we would buy all the veggies and fruit and nuts. The traders had lanterns hanging from the stalls as it got dark, it was so exciting back then and I wish I was still living in those days.

Pauline Wallis

Harlow, Market Day 1960 H22053

Washing Cars in Harlow

In the 1960s I used to wash cars in the big car park on the right of this photograph, and charged 5 shillings a car. The worst day there was when some clown of a driver went and drove over my bike, and that was that.

Barrie Brooks

"Some clown of a driver went and drove over my bike, and that was that."

Harlow, Terminus Street c1960 H22082

Fun times at the lock

My family lived in Lock Cottage beside the River Stort at Harlow from 1950, when I was 2 years old, until 1961 – my father was the lock-keeper. During the time we lived there my father rented out rowing boats and canoes for people to 'mess about on the river'. They were beautiful boats, all wood in those days, then later on kayaks came in. My father also rented out fishing permits. Most of my childhood was spent either rowing the boats or padding the canoes on the river, or fishing beside it with my sister or my mates.

Harlow, The River Stort c1955 H22012

Harlow, The Bridge at Old Harlow c1950 H22022

I spent many a long hour fishing from the towpath beside the river, and photograph H22022 (above) shows the bank where I did most of my fishing from. There used to be a very large weeping willow tree there that overhung the river, and we would cast our fishing lines underneath it as fish would congregate in the water at that spot. Just off to the left of this photograph was our garden, with a pear and apple tree, a water well, a lawn and then a vegetable garden right to the top, where the horse grips are. In those days the barges were pulled by Shire horses, not until the late 1950s did monkey boats (narrow boats) come in. Over the bridge in this view are the telephone wires where my dad once saved a swan that had got caught up in them. It broke both wings but survived, although when it got better it could not fly any more; it came down to the lock gates every single day as if to say thanks to my dad, and I've got photos of him feeding it with bread. When I was 3 I lost my toy speedboat under that bridge. It sank but was never found. I cried my eyes out over that.

Eddie Tait

Outsiders

My family moved to Cannons Green at Fyfield from London in 1953. We were viewed with some suspicion, as there were few 'outsiders' there at that time. Who were we, why had we come there? When I started at the primary school in 1956 my dad would sometimes pick me up in our car and the other kids would usually refuse a lift at first. Gradually we were accepted. Some people remember my mum not only as a dinner lady but because her Yorkshire accent was memorable. We had a great childhood there, exploring the old airfield, hanging out at the sports pavilion, mucking about in the snow in the winter, always finding ways to amuse ourselves with very few resources.

Joan Johnstone

Grippers of Chelmsford

The photograph of New Street in Chelmsford in 1920 (opposite) shows the Marconi works on the left, opposite the goods yard and cattle pens belonging to the railway on the right. It was in the railway goods yard that Grippers, the hardware store, kept their steel and iron stocks. This was delivered by train from Stratford and stored, then delivered by Grippers lorry. This was a special design made by the Dennis company with an off-set cab. This required a special starting procedure with the driver, Harry, heating the spark plugs in a methylated spirits can until it was hot and then swinging on the starting handle whilst swearing for a good 10 minutes. Grippers had a good reputation for service for many years which included employing seven blacksmiths behind the shop to make horse-shoe blanks for the British cavalry during the First World War of 1914-18. Each Quarter Day all their customers with credit accounts were entertained above the shop with beer, bread and cheese whilst they settled their accounts. The old forges have long since gone but a trip down the side alley under the famous wooden lintel may invoke some memories.

Doug Killick

> "Heating the spark plugs in a methylated spirits can until it was hot and then swinging on the starting handle whilst swearing for a good 10 minutes."

Chelmsford, New Street and the Marconi Works 1920 69027

The scoop from Grippers

I well remember Grippers the ironmonger's in Chelmsford, which was on the left-hand-side as you walked down the High Street. At the back of the store there was a counter that ran across the shop. In front of the counter were compartments with various sized nails, each in their own sections. You bought nails by the pound. The assistant used a scoop with a red handle to get the nails and weighed them in an old type Avery scales with a platform where the weights required were placed. When Grippers had its closing down sale, everything had to go. We went in there for one last look around. My wife Lola asked the assistant if the scoop was for sale, and he said "Yes". So now that scoop is the one remaining long-term memory we retain of Grippers. Now the scoop is used to get compost out of large bags while Lola pots up plants. The other ironmonger's in Chelmsford in the past was Hasler & Hance in Back Street, very nearby. I remember that shop just as well, as my grandfather, Cecil Perry, was the manager there. To a young lad these shops were full of loads of interesting things.

John Crouch

> "In front of the counter were compartments with various sized nails, each in their own sections. You bought nails by the pound."

Growing up in Cooksmill Green

I was born May 1st 1953 at Number 1 Kings Court Cottages at Cooksmill Green (near Chelmsford) to Albert and Dorrie Piddington, my dad worked for Edward Mallet at Kings Court Farm which is now known as Home Farm. My youngest sister Carole, my elder brothers John and Ken and myself all lived and grew up at 2 Kings Court Cottages. My memories of life in Cooksmill Green were of long summer days going to work with my dad at the farm, driving the tractors and working late nights getting the harvest in. My dad also looked after the stock at the farm and I remember steaming potatoes for the pigs to eat. I loved the potato harvest, spinning the potatoes with the tractor in the fields with all the people picking the spuds into those huge boxes, again working late nights to get the potatoes sorted and bagged. My good friend Neil Findlay and myself had the paper delivery round for many years in Cooksmill Green, we used an old tandem bicycle for our deliveries, we knew everybody in the village and what houses had dogs! I later attended Writtle Agricultural College and worked for Eastern Tractors in Chelmsford as an agricultural mechanic. I emigrated to Canada in April 1980 and now live and work in Grande Prairie, Alberta, where I have been a commercial helicopter pilot for 22 years now, but Cooksmill Green is still 'Home'.

Timothy Piddington

Saturday morning pictures at Loughton

I went to Saturday morning pictures at the cinema in Loughton High Road every week in the early 1960s, before it closed down in 1963. The edge of the cinema can be seen on the extreme left of this photograph (opposite). We had a club with a badge that said 'Grenadier' as it was a Grenada cinema, though the actual building had a 'Century' sign above it. There was a confectionery shop next door that sold packets of fake cigarettes – they were hollow tubes with foil at one end to look like glowing ash. We used to fill them with talcum powder and then blow it over the kids sitting in front of us in the cinema. The seats must have become very dusty! Every Christmas time we had a competition at the cinema club to make the best decoration. I won it one year but for some reason they thought I was a boy and my prize was a kit to make a toy tank! I don't really remember any particular films we saw there, the club was a social thing as much as anything else, but there was always a serial and I never quite worked out that if the hero died there wouldn't be anything on next week – was I daft, or what?

Susan Capes

> "Every Christmas time we had a competition at the cinema club to make the best decoration. I won it one year."

The Century Cinema and other memories of Loughton

My parents, brother and I moved to Loughton in 1959. My mum got a job working in the sweet shop next door to the cinema, which I think was called Barber's, and I remember having a 'Jubbly' (of 'Lovely Jubbly' fame) there. I have a vivid memory of when the cinema was demolished – I was playing in the back garden of the sweet shop and the owner's daughter and I told the workmen off and said we would fetch our dads to stop them pulling it down. After that we only had the Saturday morning 'flicks' at St Edmunds RC Church in Traps Hill to go to.

Julia Spicer

Loughton, High Road 1948 L106006

It was all countryside around Pitsea in the 1940s...

When I was born in the 1940s, the new town of Basildon was not yet built. I was born in Pitsea, when it was all countryside around there. Although my mum took me back to London after the war, I returned to Pitsea often to stay with my grandparents. It was the happiest time of my life. I particularly remember the freedom of walking across the fields and buying fresh eggs and the fun of getting the old noisy bus to Pitsea market on a Wednesday. We got the water from the well outside the back door, there was no flush lavvy inside the house, and no electric light, just oil lamps. But I was far happier than the kids nowadays.

Pat Skeels

Pitsea c1955 P145011

Basildon before the town centre was built...

My family came to Basildon in 1957 as part of the overspill from London. My late father was a toolmaker and was offered a job and a house. Money was tight and we made our own entertainment. I also remember collecting wood from the fields where the town centre now stands, and fruit picking from the cleared lots waiting for development.

When the shops of the 'new town' started being built (my memory is that Woolworth was the first opened in the first block) we would go down there to watch them being constructed.

Susan White

Basildon, Town Square c1965 B438025

Visits to Canvey Island in the 1950s and 60s

As a family, we used to visit Canvey quite often during the summers of the late 1950s and early 1960s. Getting onto Canvey from the A13 was quite stressful in those days. You had to turn at the Tarpots and follow the High Road all the way to the High Street, which meant queuing all the way, until you crossed at the level crossing at Benfleet station. This could take quite a while, as the excursion trains through to Southend meant that the level crossing gates kept coming down, holding up all the traffic. I know that when the underpass was built, later on in the 1960s, it made the journey a lot faster. We would then proceed to the seafront, where parking was allowed on what are the Millennium Gardens now, in Furtherwick Road. It used to be packed, so after I bought a motorcycle in 1959 my wife and I (she was my girlfriend then) used to go off first with a small tent (used for changing in), get parked and put up the tent next to us; then when my dad and mum arrived with the rest of the family, having followed in the car, we had a space for them to park in. Of course, to do this you had to be near the front of the car park so they could turn in.

We would take a picnic with us, and after eating it we would go for a swim, carefully avoiding the debris from the sewer outfall. After that we used to take a walk round the fairground, where we might have hotdogs or chips, and perhaps have a go at bingo and win a prize if we were lucky.

Then after a great day out we had to get off the Island, which was almost as bad as getting on. As Canvey was the nearest seaside resort to Dagenham it was very popular, and was always packed in those days. I now live on Canvey, and often hear people moaning about needing another road off the Island. We do need this, but thank goodness we don't have that 1950s' journey now, or there really would be something to have a moan about!

Sydney Claydon

Canvey Island, The Beach c1960   c237086

Days out by train to Leigh-on-Sea

In the 1950s we used to visit Leigh-on-Sea by train from Dagenham on a Sunday. After a stop at the cockle sheds for refreshment, and for us children to see the process of the boiling of the shellfish, we then walked along the seafront as far as Southend East railway station, because in those days the train home was as packed as most rush hour trains are today and we were assured of a seat on the train before it got to Southend Central station. Nowadays, my membership of Leigh-on-Sea Lions Club means I am often visiting the Old Town and still delight in sampling the produce of the seafood stalls. The view in this 1950s' photograph is still very recognisable as it is in a conservation area.

Eileen Hammond

Leigh-on-Sea, High Street c1950 L30024

I remember Southend Airport when it was just an aerodrome!

In the late 1950s we lived in Southbourne Grove at Westcliff-on-Sea near Southend, and myself and my friends used to thrash our bicycles across the fields (over the arterial road) and make our way to the back of the airport where the old engines were laid out in rows. If we were lucky, we could creep about amongst them without being caught! Probably my earliest memory was seeing the Tiger Moth biplanes flying around, some doing aerobatics. I remember being taken, as a very little boy, to see one that had come down, upside down, in the field at the end of the road where the shops were – Bridgewater Drive? I wish that I had been old enough to fly in one of those beautiful aeroplanes! Nowadays we can book a joy ride in one for a treat.

Colin Hayes

Southend, The Airport c1955 S155041

Wonderful days out at Southend

I remember travelling to Southend with my family in the 1950s on a steam train from London. My sister and I used to put our heads out of the windows and when we sat down our faces would be black with soot from the smoke of the train, and our mum had to wipe us clean with her hanky. When we arrived at Southend it was off to the beach for a paddle and a play, and then a ride on the boats in the boating lake. At lunchtime we walked up the hill to have our lunch of pie and mash, or fish and chips, with a Rossi ice-cream for afters. In the afternoon we would get on a boat for an excursion to the Isle of Sheppey, and then return to Southend and spend the rest of the day in the Kursaal. My fondest memory of the Kursaal was the bowl slide, where you were taken to the top of the slide by an electric chair and then given a coconut mat to sit on whilst you slid down. At the end of the slide was a big wooden bowl to catch the riders in – it was such a thrill. I remember how lovely and shiny the wood on the slide looked through constant use. At the end of the day we headed back to the train station, stopping along the way to buy seafood sold in straw bags, but as you walked along, the liquid would seep through the bag! Those were the days. How I long for my grandchildren to be able to ride on that beautiful slide, but sadly it is now long gone.

Jan Rennie

Southend-on-Sea, The Boating Lake and Pier Hill c1950 S155020

Holidays at Shoebury Hall Farm Camp at Shoeburyness in the 1950s and 60s

This camp site at Shoebury Hall Farm was owned by Captain H R Townsend RN and his wife, Margaret I think. They were like the country squire and his family. Their house was between the church and the camp site. Captain Townsend could often be seen riding round the camp on his bike making sure that all was well and the campers were not getting up to any mischief. The Townsends were treated with great respect and they reciprocated.

This photograph shows 'Jellicoe Square' on the camp site, looking north – I recognized it from the chalet in the corner and St Andrew's Church in the background. This is where my parents had their caravan from about 1958 to 1967. Mum and Dad had been camping at the site since before the Second World War, following their marriage in 1935. In those early days the campsite was mostly for tents, and we had to be careful when coming back late at night not to trip over the guy ropes as there was no lighting on the site whatsoever, only faint glows from the Tilley lamps in the tents.

The campsite was pretty basic then not like today's caravan sites. The toilets were situated in two blocks, one on the east side of the camp and the other on the west, and it was a fairly large site so a visit could entail a long walk! We used to wash in our shed next to our caravan. There was no running water, one had to go to one of the taps scattered about the site and bring water back in a metal jug, hot and cold. I would often go and get the water from about the age of ten. I learnt never to spill it, especially the hot.

Cooking and lighting were by calor gas, there was no electricity. We did have a camp shop that sold all you could want really, bread, bacon, ham, cheese, milk, sweets, comics and ice-cream. In the evening one of the men from the shop would go round the site selling newspapers, shouting 'Evening News' and 'Standard'. In the 1960s at the start of the Beatles and Rolling Stones era they even got a jukebox in the shop, much to the annoyance of the staff working there as we teenagers were forever grouped around it playing the same stuff over and over again. We never vandalised anything or caused trouble though. We dared not, and anyway, we didn't want to.

The camp was closed in the early 1970s I think, and its site is now a housing estate.

Alan Perry

Shoeburyness, Shoebury Hall Farm Camp c1955   S275029

Memories of Burnham-on Crouch from 1948 onwards

Our family moved to Burnham-on-Crouch from Wimbledon (Raynes Park) in late 1948, when I was 4. Our new home was 34 Lillian Road. We arrived like pioneers of the Wild West in the back of my father's employer's canvas-covered Ford truck; Mum and Dad sat in the cab with the baby brother, and my two elder brothers and me were in the back, with our two cats. Being Londoners we were not too well liked by the locals, such was the attitude in those days, and life was hard and tough for the first few years. In early 1949 I had fight with a boy from Queens Road on the first playing field, where the fair and circus used to set up, but this lad and I then went on to become best mates, right up until his death in 2005.

My second eldest brother and me would walk for miles during the summer holidays, either along the river bank to the marshes, Dammelwick, Flakehouse and across to Stoney Hills via Newman's farm or upstream towards Wickford, stopping at Fanbridge, or cutting over land to Althorne or Southminster where we would try to thumb a lift from one of the rare cars that were on the roads. I remember one Sunday afternoon my brother and I went swimming on the ebb tide and my brother was swept off the causeway on the New Beach and I stood helpless as I watched him drowning. He had gone down twice, about 150 yards from shore, when a Mrs Mary Harding, a local mother of a boy in my class, ran past, dived in, swam out to him and brought him back. She had saved his life and he was a very lucky boy, as the Crouch is a killer as sadly some families can testify.

When I was about 10 years old we used to work during the school holidays on Jack Clear's farm at the top of Foundry Lane, which was then a dirt road lined by trees and hedges one side and the foundry on the other. Almost everybody in town used to listen for the foundry bell, which rang five times a day: at start of work, at 10.00am for the morning break, at dinner start and end, and finish of work at 17.30pm. They all worked their days around that bell, you could hear it for miles. A few years later I used to help the Co-op milkman, a great bloke who taught me to drive in return for my efforts to hinder him. Our house was at the back and side of the Co-op and milk was delivered in bulk to their yard where it was loaded on to two milkfloats, and the second half of the round was stored in the garage. We would load the 1 ton float and I, as a 14 year old, would drive to the starting point at Creeksea.

We went to school in Devonshire Road and I went to the new school in Southminster Road in 1958 to 1959. On leaving school I started work at E H Bentall & Co in Heybridge, leaving Burnham at 06.30am and getting home at 19.30pm. That was a long day for a 15-year-old, but that was what was expected of the young in those days. *Malcolm Bowen*

Burnham-on-Crouch, High Street c1960 B325091

Wickham Bishops – a real English village

In 1948 my family moved to Wickham Bishops, near Witham, where my parents helped friends run the village Post Office Stores. The stores sold everything – stamps, paraffin (you brought your own can and it was filled from a barrel at the back), vinegar (as for the paraffin, it came from a barrel out the back), cheese portions cut from huge cheeses wrapped in linen, and loose flour and pulses which even as a five-year-old I was allowed to put into blue sugar-paper bags to be weighed. Sweets were still rationed in those days, following the war, and broken biscuits were popular. My mother and her friend went once a year to order skirts, blouses, frocks and underwear for the shop from the London warehouses. Toys that came into the shop for Christmas stock were not packaged in plastic like nowadays, so I got the first go with them!

There was a village pantomime every year in which all the local characters took part, some of them glamorous in fishnet tights as characters like Dandini or hideous in wigs and false chests as the Ugly Sisters. There was also a Christmas party for everyone who wanted to go, with proper games in which all the adults made fools of themselves, like trying to whistle the National Anthem after eating a cream cracker or rushing round chairs till the music stopped. I remember many of the village people from those days, great characters all of them, some wealthy, some poor. We were quite poor but it was post-war and we weren't alone in that. I was ill a lot of the time with asthma and one kind family lent me their children's toys to play with; I loved the Lego as I had never been given such a toy before, being female.

My fondest memory of the village is of a family who lived in converted railway carriages whilst they built themselves a house – I thought it was wonderful having one room after another and lots of windows.

We moved to Great Totham when I was 10, but Wickham Bishops remains always in my memory as my childhood home.

Carol Argyris

Childhood memories of Hatfield Peverel

I lived at Number 3 The Terrace, Station Road, Hatfield Peverel and started at the local school in 1945. My father worked for Lord Raleigh at Bury Farm and also at Termitts Farm. As a lad I worked for Mr Oliver, the local baker, on a Saturday morning, we used to make the bread early in the morning and then Mr Oliver would deliver the bread with his horse and cart. I would follow him on my bike, with a basket on my arm, and he gave me the bread to take to customers' houses. On Saturday afternoon I worked for Bob Sorrell the butcher on the corner of Bury Lane, again delivering meat on my trade bike with a basket on the front. After that it was time to scrub out the freezers before finishing off in the shop.

In the wartime years I can also remember the prisoners of war when they were at the dairy, they made us 'pecking chickens' on a board, like a table tennis bat with strings, when it moved it looked as though the chickens were pecking up their food.

Philip Crane

FRANCIS FRITH

PIONEER VICTORIAN PHOTOGRAPHER

Francis Frith, founder of the world-famous photographic archive, was a complex and multi-talented man. A devout Quaker and a highly successful Victorian businessman, he was philosophical by nature and pioneering in outlook. By 1855 he had already established a wholesale grocery business in Liverpool, and sold it for the astonishing sum of £200,000, which is the equivalent today of over £15,000,000. Now in his thirties, and captivated by the new science of photography, Frith set out on a series of pioneering journeys up the Nile and to the Near East.

INTRIGUE AND EXPLORATION

He was the first photographer to venture beyond the sixth cataract of the Nile. Africa was still the mysterious 'Dark Continent', and Stanley and Livingstone's historic meeting was a decade into the future. The conditions for picture taking confound belief. He laboured for hours in his wicker dark-room in the sweltering heat of the desert, while the volatile chemicals fizzed dangerously in their trays. Back in London he exhibited his photographs and was 'rapturously cheered' by members of the Royal Society. His reputation as a photographer was made overnight.

VENTURE OF A LIFE-TIME

By the 1870s the railways had threaded their way across the country, and Bank Holidays and half-day Saturdays had been made obligatory by Act of Parliament. All of a sudden the working man and his family were able to enjoy days out, take holidays, and see a little more of the world.

With typical business acumen, Francis Frith foresaw that these new tourists would enjoy having souvenirs to commemorate their days out. For the next thirty years he travelled the country by train and by pony and trap, producing fine photographs of seaside resorts and beauty spots that were keenly bought by millions of Victorians. These prints were painstakingly pasted into family albums and pored over during the dark nights of winter, rekindling precious memories of summer excursions. Frith's studio was soon supplying retail shops all over the country, and by 1890 F Frith & Co had become the greatest specialist photographic publishing company in the world, with over 2,000 sales outlets, and pioneered the picture postcard.

FRANCIS FRITH'S LEGACY

Francis Frith had died in 1898 at his villa in Cannes, his great project still growing. By 1970 the archive he created contained over a third of a million pictures showing 7,000 British towns and villages.

Frith's legacy to us today is of immense significance and value, for the magnificent archive of evocative photographs he created provides a unique record of change in the cities, towns and villages throughout Britain over a century and more. Frith and his fellow studio photographers revisited locations many times down the years to update their views, compiling for us an enthralling and colourful pageant of British life and character.

We are fortunate that Frith was dedicated to recording the minutiae of everyday life. For it is this sheer wealth of visual data, the painstaking chronicle of changes in dress, transport, street layouts, buildings, housing and landscape that captivates us so much today, offering us a powerful link with the past and with the lives of our ancestors.

Computers have now made it possible for Frith's many thousands of images to be accessed almost instantly. The archive offers every one of us an opportunity to examine the places where we and our families have lived and worked down the years. Its images, depicting our shared past, are now bringing pleasure and enlightenment to millions around the world a century and more after his death.

For further information visit: www.francisfrith.com

INTERIOR DECORATION

Frith's photographs can be seen framed and as giant wall murals in thousands of pubs, restaurants, hotels, banks, retail stores and other public buildings throughout Britain. These provide interesting and attractive décor, generating strong local interest and acting as a powerful reminder of gentler days in our increasingly busy and frenetic world.

FRITH PRODUCTS

All Frith photographs are available as prints and posters in a variety of different sizes and styles. In the UK we also offer a range of other gift and stationery products illustrated with Frith photographs, although many of these are not available for delivery outside the UK – see our web site for more information on the products available for delivery in your country.

THE INTERNET

Over 100,000 photographs of Britain can be viewed and purchased on the Frith web site. The web site also includes memories and reminiscences contributed by our customers, who have personal knowledge of localities and of the people and properties depicted in Frith photographs. If you wish to learn more about a specific town or village you may find these reminiscences fascinating to browse. Why not add your own comments if you think they would be of interest to others? See **www.francisfrith.com**

PLEASE HELP US BRING FRITH'S PHOTOGRAPHS TO LIFE

Our authors do their best to recount the history of the places they write about. They give insights into how particular towns and villages developed, they describe the architecture of streets and buildings, and they discuss the lives of famous people who lived there. But however knowledgeable our authors are, the story they tell is necessarily incomplete.

Frith's photographs are so much more than plain historical documents. They are living proofs of the flow of human life down the generations. They show real people at real moments in history; and each of those people is the son or daughter of someone, the brother or sister, aunt or uncle, grandfather or grandmother of someone else. All of them lived, worked and played in the streets depicted in Frith's photographs.

We would be grateful if you would give us your insights into the places shown in our photographs: the streets and buildings, the shops, businesses and industries. Post your memories of life in those streets on the Frith website: what it was like growing up there, who ran the local shop and what shopping was like years ago; if your workplace is shown tell us about your working day and what the building is used for now. Read other visitors' memories and reconnect with your shared local history and heritage. With your help more and more Frith photographs can be brought to life, and vital memories preserved for posterity, and for the benefit of historians in the future.

Wherever possible, we will try to include some of your comments in future editions of our books. Moreover, if you spot errors in dates, titles or other facts, please let us know, because our archive records are not always completely accurate—they rely on 140 years of human endeavour and hand-compiled records. You can email us using the contact form on the website.

Thank you!

For further information, trade, or author enquiries
please contact us at the address below:

**The Francis Frith Collection, 6 Oakley Business Park,
Wylye Road, Dinton, Wiltshire SP3 5EU.**
Tel: +44 (0)1722 716 376 Fax: +44 (0)1722 716 881
e-mail: sales@francisfrith.co.uk **www.francisfrith.com**